YOU ARE MAJESTIC AS FUCK

YOU
ARE THE
BADDASSIEST
BADASS
IN ALL OF
BADASSIA

YOU ARE FUCKING AWESOME

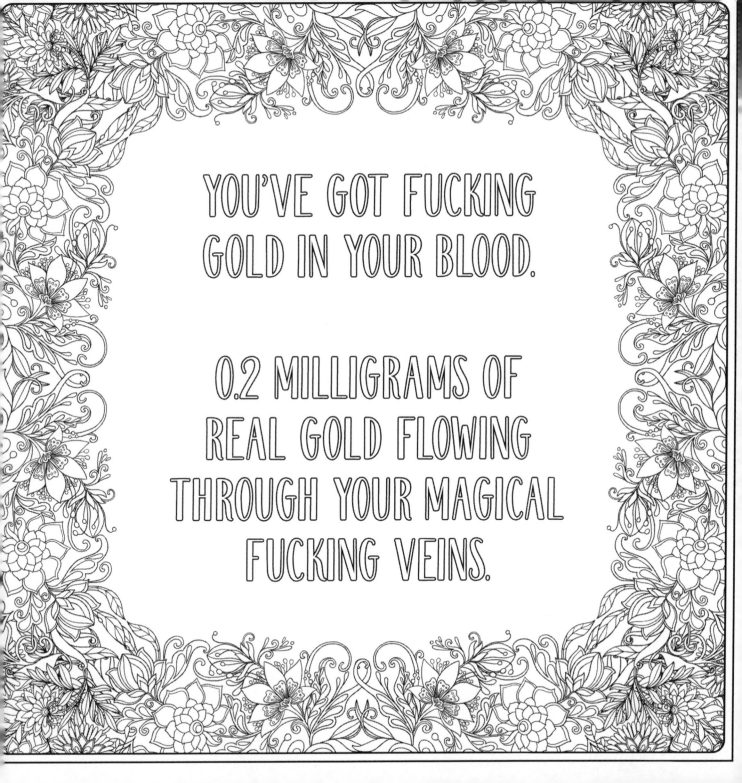

YOU'VE GOT FUCKING GOLD IN YOUR BLOOD.

0.2 MILLIGRAMS OF REAL GOLD FLOWING THROUGH YOUR MAGICAL FUCKING VEINS.

YOU'RE A GODDAMN DRAGON INSIDE

YOU ARE A
RADIANT BALL
OF BEAUTY
& SHIT

YOU ARE A FUCKING LION. RAWR.

YOUR SPECTACULAR FUCKING BRAIN IS THE MOST COMPLEX OBJECT IN THE KNOWN UNIVERSE. HOLY SHIT.

YOU CAN TRANSFORM INTO ANYTHING YOU WANT YOU DAZZLING FUCKING BUTTERFLY

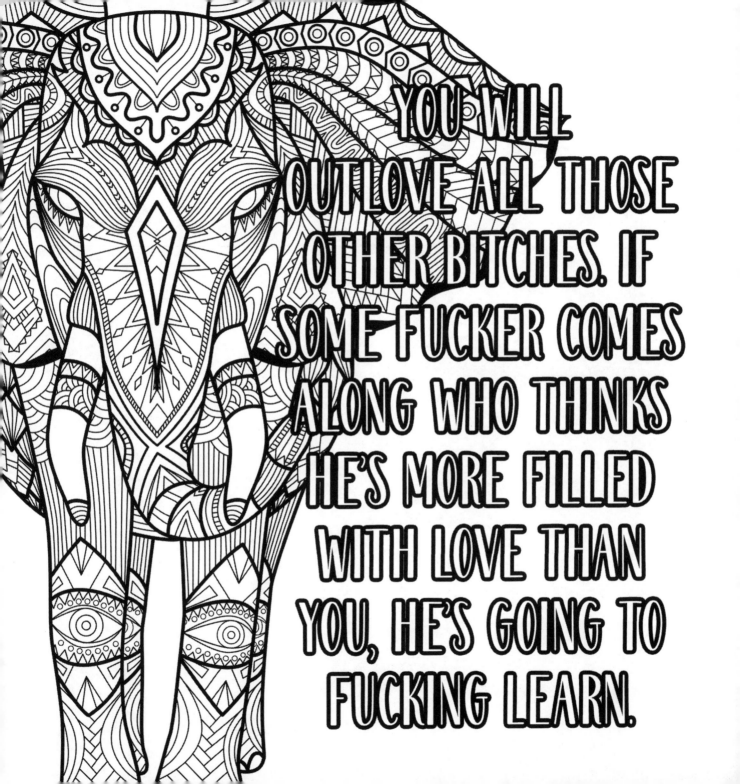

YOU WILL OUTLOVE ALL THOSE OTHER BITCHES. IF SOME FUCKER COMES ALONG WHO THINKS HE'S MORE FILLED WITH LOVE THAN YOU, HE'S GOING TO FUCKING LEARN.

DO
WHAT
MAKES
YOU
FUCKING
HAPPY

64474567R00025

Made in the USA
Lexington, KY
09 June 2017